EMERGING
NATIONS

RUSSIA

PHILIP STEELE

A+

Smart Apple Media

EMERGING NATIONS

RUSSIA

A⁺
Smart Apple Media

Published by Smart Apple Media, an imprint of Black Rabbit Books
P.O. Box 3263, Mankato, Minnesota 56002
www.blackrabbitbooks.com

Published by arrangement with the Watts Publishing Group LTD, London.

Cataloging-in-Publication Data is available from the Library of Congress
ISBN 978-1-59920-989-0 (library binding)
ISBN 978-1-62588-604-0 (eBook)

Series Editor: Julia Bird
Series Advisor: Emma Epsley, geography teacher and consultant
Series Design: sprout.uk.com

Photo credits:
Olga A/Shutterstock: 31t. Bryan & Cherry Alexander/Arctic Photo: 11. Goran Bogicevic/Shutterstock: 9b. Cescassawin/Dreamstime: front cover b, 3b. Danilov/Shutterstock: 27bl.Dmitry Ersler/Shutterstock: 28. Jack F/Dreamstime: 19b. Alexei Fateev/Alamy: 12. Iakov Filimonov/Shutterstock: 6b. Sue Flood/Getty Images: 23. Oleg Fokin/Shutterstock: 7b. FotograFF/Shutterstock: 20. Anton Gvozdokov/Shutterstock: 13cl, 13cr. ID1974/Shutterstock: 17t. ITAR-TASS/Alamy: 14, 41,43t. Julia 161/Dreamstime: 26, 39tr. Martti Kainulainen/Rex Features: 19t. Peter Kirilov/Shutterstock: 35b. Pavel L Photo and Video/Shutterstock: front cover t, 3t, 10t, 30. Pavel Losevsky/Dreamstime: 33b. Ludovic Maisant/Corbis: 38. Anna Martynova/Dreamstime: 15. Ian Masterton/Alamy: 33t. Michael Nicholson/Corbis: 8b. Nordroden/Dreamstime: 24. Oledjio/Shutterstock: 18. Olemac/Shutterstock: 43b. Sergey Petrov/Shutterstock: 34. PhotoXpress/Zuma Press/Alamy: 27t. Ekaterina Pokrovsky/Dreamstime: 36. Valeriya Popova/Shutterstock: 13b. Prysha/Dreamstime: 37. RIA/Novosti/Alamy: 27br. RIA/Novosti/Topfoto: 39tl. rm/Shutterstock: 40. Andrey Rudakov/Bloomberg/Getty Images: 16. Shamuker Rusian/Photoshot: 31b. Mircea Preda Struteanu/Dreamstime: 22. Toxawww/Dreamstime: 39bl. Raluca Tudor/Dreamstime: 32. Vadiuhaps/Shutterstock: 17b. Vasily Vishnevskiy/Dreamstime: 25. VLADJ55/Shutterstock: 13t. Lilyana Vynogradova/Shutterstock: 39br. Westend6/Gmbh/Alamy: 42. withGod/Shutterstock: 21b. Yuri4u80/Dreamstime: 9t. yykkaa/Shutterstock: 21t. Zuma Press/Alamy: 29, 35t.

Printed in the United States by CG Book Printers
North Mankato, Minnesota

PO 1721
3-2015

987654321

RUSSIA

CONTENTS

CHAPTER 1

INTRODUCING RUSSIA
THE NEW RUSSIA

On May 25, Russian teenagers are celebrating "the Last Bell"—the end of their final term at school. The boys dress in smart suits. The girls wear formal black dresses with sashes and lacy ribbons in their hair. Presentations are given to teachers with speeches, laughter, and tears.

CHILDREN OF CHANGE

When today's teenagers leave school, they face a very different future from their parents and grandparents. In the last hundred years Russia has experienced rule by an emperor, two world wars, revolutions, civil war, communism, and capitalism. Even the national borders have altered. Great social and economic changes have swept across the land. Today, Russia is more prosperous than at any time in its history. But what kind of nation has it become? How would today's teenagers like it to be in the future?

A GIANT NATION

Russia is the largest nation on Earth. It occupies about one-eighth of the planet's surface. What happens there affects almost every part of the world. With an area of 6.6 million square miles (17 million sq km), it is about 1.8 times the size of the United States. Russia's bleak, deep-frozen tundra borders the Arctic coast. Farther south are the great forests known as taiga. In the far south, grassy steppes are bordered by high mountains. Russian summers can be warm and sunny, but the winters are snowy and bitterly cold.

FROM EUROPE TO ASIA

The Russian Federation covers nine time zones and straddles two continents. European Russia occupies the vast plain that stretches from Central Europe to the Ural Mountains. The Caucasus Mountains and the coasts of the Black Sea and the Caspian Sea are in the south. Elbrus is Europe's highest mountain peak, soaring to 18,500 feet (5,600 m). Asian Russia extends all the way from the Urals to the volcanoes of the Pacific Rim. This region of plains and plateaus is known as Siberia. It is crossed by three of the ten longest rivers in the world: the Yenisey, Ob-Irtysh, and Amur. Baikal is world's deepest lake and may hold as much as 20 percent of the world's fresh water.

School graduates in the city of Vladimir line up for the "Last Bell" ceremony.

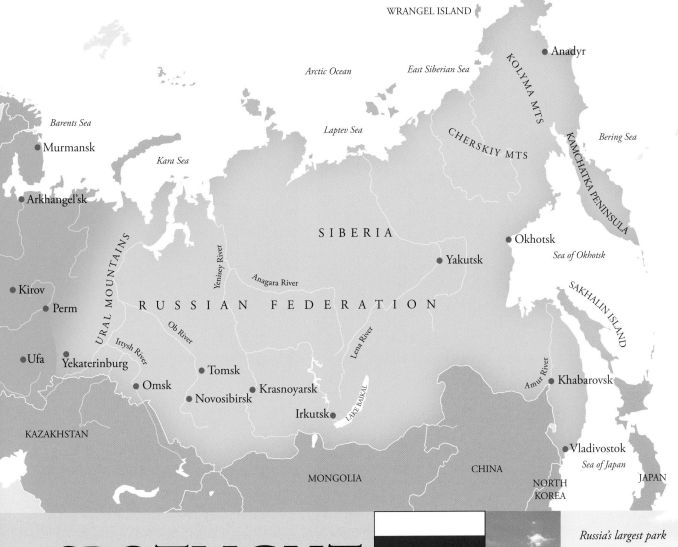

WRANGEL ISLAND

Arctic Ocean

East Siberian Sea

• Anadyr

KOLYMA MTS

Barents Sea

Laptev Sea

CHERSKIY MTS

KAMCHATKA PENINSULA

Bering Sea

• Murmansk

Kara Sea

SIBERIA

Sea of Okhotsk

• Okhotsk

• Arkhangel'sk

URAL MOUNTAINS

Yenisey River

Anagara River

• Yakutsk

RUSSIAN FEDERATION

SAKHALIN ISLAND

• Kirov

• Perm

Ob River

Lena River

Irtysh River

Amur River

• Ufa

• Yekaterinburg

• Khabarovsk

• Tomsk

• Omsk

• Krasnoyarsk

LAKE BAIKAL

• Novosibirsk

Irkutsk •

KAZAKHSTAN

• Vladivostok

Sea of Japan

MONGOLIA

CHINA

NORTH KOREA

JAPAN

SPOTLIGHT ON RUSSIA

FULL NAME: Russian Federation
• SHORT NAME: Russia • AREA: 6.6 million square miles (17 million sq km)
• POPULATION: 143 million
• CAPITAL: Moscow (10.5 million)
• SECOND CITY: St. Petersburg (4.8 million)
• LONGEST RIVER: Yenisey 3,440 miles (5,540 km) • HIGHEST MOUNTAIN: Elbrus 18,500 feet (5,633 m) • RESOURCES: Oil, natural gas, coal, gold, iron ore, chromium, nickel, copper, tin, lead, phosphates, timber, fish

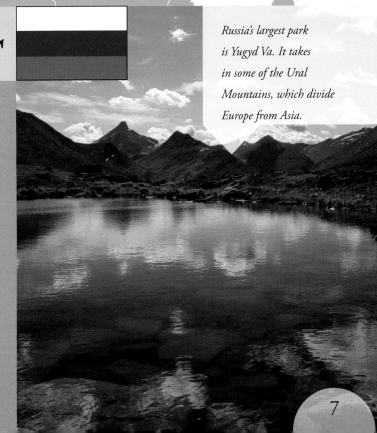

Russia's largest park is Yugyd Va. It takes in some of the Ural Mountains, which divide Europe from Asia.

7

PEOPLE AND NATION

BIG HISTORY

In 2012, President Vladimir Putin made a speech about Russia's future. He called on people to seek guidance from their country's past. Russia's eventful history certainly offers many lessons.

THE AGE OF EMPIRE

Russia's story began in the Middle Ages (fifth to fifteenth centuries AD) when a patchwork of cities and small states grew up in the lands of the Eastern Slavs. Over time, the most powerful city became Moscow, capital of Muscovy. Its rulers forged all Russia into a single empire. Over the centuries, this empire expanded westward, southward, and eastward across Siberia. Many of Russia's emperors, or tsars, were harsh rulers. While other European peoples were gaining more rights and freedoms, Russia's peasants remained serfs.

REVOLUTION AND CIVIL WAR

Revolutions broke out in 1905 and in 1917, during World War I. A group called the Bolsheviks, led by Vladimir Ilyich Lenin, seized power. They founded the Russian Communist Party, which aimed to give power to the workers. The ruling tsar, Nicholas II, was shot and killed in 1918. In a civil war that lasted until 1922, the communist Red Army defeated their opponents, who were known as the Whites. A new state was formed as the Union of Soviet Socialist Republics (USSR, or Soviet Union).

Lenin (1870–1924) was a revolutionary. His ideas influenced world politics throughout the 20th century.

Joseph Dzhugashvili, or Stalin (1878–1953) was a ruthless, dictatorial leader.

COLD WAR AND REFORM

After the war, Soviet power dominated Eastern Europe. The Cold War, from 1945 to 1991, was a period of tension between the Soviet Union on one side and the United States and Western Europe on the other.

Political reform followed Stalin's death in 1953. But it was not until Mikhail Gorbachev was in power (1985–91) that Russia really began to change. Gorbachev's aims included *perestroika* (restructuring the system) and *glasnost* (openness), and relations with the West began to thaw. In 1991, a conservative group within the Communist Party tried to force Gorbachev from power. They failed, but the Soviet Union collapsed. Fourteen regions broke away to become independent nations. The new Russian Federation, with a multiparty political system and a capitalist economy was born.

During the Cold War, both sides were armed with nuclear weapons and developed rocket technology.

STALIN'S RUSSIA

Lenin died in 1924. Joseph Stalin, cunning politician, soon won control. He pushed through reforms in industry and farming, at great human cost. Millions of people died in a famine in 1932–33. Many people were murdered or sent to grim labor camps. At the start of World War II in 1939, Russia and Germany agreed not to attack each other. But in 1940, Adolf Hitler ordered the invasion of the Soviet Union. The extraordinary Russian resistance and counterattack was crucial to Germany's defeat in 1945. This "Great Patriotic War" is still commemorated across Russia every May 9.

MEET THE PEOPLE

Russians buy fresh food at a local market in Preobrazhensky in Moscow.

As you travel across Russia, the forests seem to stretch on forever. Where are all the people? The population density is one of the lowest in the world with just 25 people per square mile (3 sq km).

THE RUSSIANS

Русские, pronounced *Russkiye*, means the Russians. The Russian language is written in a Cyrillic script. Ethnic Russians, a Slavic people from European Russia, make up about 80 percent of the national population. Over the ages, they have also settled in many other parts of the former Russian empire and the Soviet Union, as well as overseas.

HARSH TERRAIN

Russia may be the world's largest country, but its population of 143 million is barely 11 percent of that in neighboring China. One reason for this is the difficulty of making a home in Russia's harsher regions. In Siberia, winter temperatures can plunge to −76°F (−60°C), and permafrost makes the deeper soil as hard as iron. Eight out of ten Russians live in the west where the land is better for farming and big cities are thriving.

UNITED OR DIVIDED?

In some parts of the country, non-Russians outnumber ethnic Russians. These regions are referred to as republics. The local languages may be used as well as Russian for schooling and government. The law guarantees the rights of minorities. In practice, ethnic tensions are quite common. Some of Russia's minorities have experienced centuries of conquest or resettlement and racism. Old grievances have been stirred up since the break up of the old Soviet Union.

CHECHEN WAR

After the Soviet Union collapsed in 1991, the people of Chechnya demanded independence, as did many bordering regions. The government refused and sent in the army in a campaign against Chechen guerrillas and civilians. A brutal Second Chechen War began in 1999 and lasted 10 years. This led to terrorist attacks by Chechens in Russian cities. Today, the war is over, but it has left lasting bitterness.

The Nenets have lived in Russia's frozen northwest for thousands of years.

PART OF THE WHOLE

The Russian Federation is comprised of over 180 ethnic groups in all. Ukrainians, who are Slavs like the Russians, make up about 2 percent of the national population. Turkic peoples, such as the Tatars, Bashkir, and Chuvash, account for over 6 percent. Most of these minority peoples lead much the same kind of lives as ethnic Russians. However, some small Arctic groups, such as the Nenets and Sami, work to keep up their own traditions of herding reindeer or hunting and fishing for a living.

People who live in Moscow (Moskva) are called Muscovites. Their city changes dramatically with the seasons. In the heat of summer, people can stroll or sun themselves in the leafy parks. In the snowy winter months, pedestrians need to wrap up and wear furry or woolen hats while traffic makes its way over the ice and slush.

RUSSIA'S BIGGEST CITY

Moscow is the powerhouse of the Russian Federation. It is the capital city, the hub of political power, and a center of business and industry. It is by far the biggest city, with a population of over 10.5 million.

THE KREMLIN

The Kremlin is the heart of Moscow. It is a medieval stronghold beside the Moscow River. Within its red walls are the golden domes of cathedrals, the tombs of the tsars, palaces, treasure houses, government buildings, and the official residence of the president. East of the Kremlin is Red Square, which is used for grand military parades, concerts, and many national events.

BUILDINGS

Ring roads divide the city into zones. Some architecture dates back to the time of the tsars, and many public buildings were built when Stalin was still in power. Grand railway terminals sit side by side with dreary high-rise housing blocks and factories from the 1960s and 1970s. Glassy skyscrapers have been built in recent years.

WEEKEND HOMES

Many of Moscow's rich own luxurious country houses, or *dachas*, in the forests around Moscow. Less wealthy city-dwellers also have their own dachas—shacks, summer houses, and small cottages with vegetable plots outside the city limits. These are intended for recreation only, but some Muscovites move into them and rent out their city flats to make more money.

Snow is cleared from Red Square, which is next to St. Basil's cathedral. About 15,000 snowplows and trucks clear the streets during Moscow's long, fierce winters.

Moscow's Kremlin has been at the center of Russian history for centuries.

The changing of the guard takes place at the Tomb of the Unknown Soldier. An eternal flame commemorates the troops who died in the Great Patriotic War (see page 9).

Moscow's new business district overlooks the wide Moscow River.

Arbat Street is one of the oldest in Moscow. It is popular with tourists, who enjoy its entertainers, souvenir and antique shops, street artists, and fast food stalls.

POLITICS AND POWER

*Russian president
Vladimir Putin.*

The politics of today's Russia has been shaped mainly by two men: Boris Yeltsin and Vladimir Putin.

TIME OF TRANSITION

Boris Yeltsin was the elected president from 1991 to 1999 during a chaotic period of great political change in Russia. Yeltsin took on personal powers, such as sending in tanks to attack the Russian parliament in 1993. His shock economic reforms deprived millions of people of the basic welfare that had been provided by the Soviet state. On the other hand, a few people became extremely rich and powerful and were nicknamed oligarchs (members of a ruling elite). Crime and corruption flourished during this time.

PUTIN'S RUSSIA

Vladimir Putin, a former secret police chief, followed Yeltsin as president from 2001 to 2008. From 2008 to 2012 Putin swapped jobs with Prime Minister Dmitry Medvedev before being reelected to the presidency in 2012. Under President Putin, the Russian economy has improved and stabilized. This has brought Putin widespread support. He is seen as a tough guy who gets things done and stands up for Russia in international politics. He is fond of public relations stunts and likes to present himself as a heroic man of action.

CRITICS

Putin's critics see him as an authoritarian leader and one who likes to intimidate opponents and clamp down on protest. He is accused of fixing elections and failing to tackle corruption. There is a great gap between rich and poor, and oligarchs can still remain extremely wealthy—unless they fall out with Putin. Many now complain that Putin has too much personal power, and protests are growing.

HOW IT WORKS

Russia's president is head of state, while its prime minister heads the government. The Federal Assembly's upper house is called the Federation Council. It has two delegates from each of Russia's 83 provinces, regions, and federal cities. The lower house is the State Duma, or parliament, whose 450 deputies are elected for five-year terms.

Voting takes place for the 2011 elections to the State Duma.

The voting age is 18. Under the old Soviet system, representatives could be chosen only from the Communist Party. However, in the last Duma election in 2011, seven political parties were represented. The biggest winner was Putin's conservative United Russia party. The Communist Party of the Russian Federation came in second. The social democratic coalition called A Just Russia was third. The ultra-nationalist Liberal Democratic Party of Russia came fourth.

15

CHAPTER 2:
LAND AND WORK
MONEY MATTERS

Workers come off shift at the Sibirginsky mine in Siberia. This mine supplies coal for the steel industry.

In 1998, Russia was on the verge of economic collapse. Now, it is possible that it could become Europe's top economy by 2030. What can explain such a rapid increase?

OIL AND GAS GIANT

The answer lies under the ground. Russia currently ranks second in the world for oil production and first for natural gas. Gazprom, a gigantic company that is 50 percent owned by the Russian state, transports more gas than any other company in the world. International pipelines bring political power and profits. However, Vladimir Putin's drive to control business within Russia for his own political purposes, or a failure to deal with corruption, could eventually derail the probability of prosperity.

MINERAL WEALTH

The Russian soil is a treasure chest of other useful resources. These include coal, iron ore, gold, diamonds, chromium, nickel, copper, tin, lead, and phosphates. But it can be difficult to mine or drill in Russia's harshest regions, and it is expensive to transport minerals over huge distances.

WHAT DOES RUSSIA PRODUCE?

Russia's trading partners include China, Japan, the European Union, and Turkey. Russia's factories and mills turn out heavy machinery, as well as armaments, aircraft, ships, cars and trucks, chemicals, cotton textiles, and household appliances. A high-tech innovations center for projects as varied as biomedical research and space technology is being developed at Skolvoko, on the outskirts of Moscow.

Workers on the production line at a factory run by the Moscow Brewing Company.

BRICS

Along with Brazil, India, China, and South Africa, Russia is part of the BRICS group. These governments want to champion developing economies around the world. All of these nations have economies that have been growing very fast. They are all large countries, too, either by area or population (or both). However, they all have very different political systems. Ultimately, this may make it difficult for them to share economic programs.

MAKING A LIVING

About 27 percent of Russian laborers are industrial workers and nearly 10 percent work on the land. The remaining workers provide services and include teachers, doctors, cleaners, cooks, and office workers. Russia is unusual, as it has a standard rate of income tax for all, very low at 13 percent. As some business people make huge fortunes in the new Russia, a wealthy middle class is emerging in Moscow and St. Petersburg. However, about 1.3 million Russians, many of them working in public services, earn only the national minimum wage. In 2013, this was set at $182 per month (6,245 rubles) in the national currency. That does not cover the basic costs of living, so many poor people struggle to get by.

Working with wood. More than 20 percent of the world's forestry resources are found in the Russian Federation.

LIVING IN CITIES

Today, seven out of ten Russians live in cities or towns. The biggest cities are Moscow, St. Petersburg, Novosibirsk, Yekaterinburg, and Nizhny Novgorod.

BEYOND MOSCOW

In a country with such icy winters, it can be very costly to keep roads and housing in remote towns in good condition. The government plans to tackle this infrastructure problem in the coming years. Too many towns still depend on only one kind of industry. If a mine or a factory is shut down, there may be no alternative plan. Jobs are less secure today than they were under Soviet rule.

HOUSING NEW AND OLD

City housing reveals just how much everyday life in Russia has changed over the years. In Soviet days, all housing was owned by the state. Some people still live in the blocks of single-family flats known as *khrushchevki*, which were constructed when Nikita Khruschev was the Soviet leader between 1953 and 1964. Built quickly and cheaply, the flats are short of space. Generally, the sitting room doubles as a bedroom by night. Many *krushchevki* are now being demolished to make room for new homes.

These flats called khrushchevki *were built as a temporary answer to Russia's housing shortage. They were designed only to last about 35 years.*

HOMELESS

St. Petersburg, called Leningrad during the Soviet era, is a beautiful city of bridges, canals, and rivers. However, it shares an ugly problem with many other cities across Russia and around the world—homelessness.

- How many people live in St. Petersburg? As Russia's second largest city, it has a population of about 4.8 million.

- How many of homeless? Every night more than 30,000 people sleep on the streets of St. Petersburg.

- Why do people have nowhere to go? Some have alcohol or drug problems. Some are former prisoners. Many are children—often orphans. Across the Russian Federation, as many as a million children are without a proper home.

- Who helps them? Many charities provide food and temporary shelter.

SPREADING OUT

Town planning is no longer controlled as tightly. This allows new low-rise developments to grow in the suburbs—often around metro stations. In turn, these encourage more localized businesses, shops, and outdoor markets. The most luxurious new apartment blocks in central city districts can be afforded only by the very rich.

Homeless people face a tough existence on the streets of Russia's cities.

Nevsky Prospekt is the main street in St. Petersburg. It is always crowded with shoppers and tourists.

RURAL RUSSIA

Life is peaceful on a summer day in the countryside. However, traditional village life is under threat across Russia.

When Russians leave the city streets for a weekend at their dacha, they may be looking for a return to their rural past. Memories of the countryside might include traditional timber houses, dusty farm roads, and the scent of lilac blossom on summer days, or autumn forays into the forest to pick wild mushrooms or berries.

VILLAGES AND FARMS

Rural Russia still exists, but it has taken many hard knocks over the years. As cities grow ever more powerful, rural communities are disappearing. Village schools and local hospitals are closing. In 2010, about 3,000 villages were abandoned across Russia. Village life changed greatly in the Soviet era. Family farms were reorganized as part of state-owned farms or collectives. Today, another age of change has swept across Russia. Food can be produced on household plots and small peasant farms or on huge estates run by corporations. Farmers from other countries have moved into the Russian market by buying up land for farming pigs or growing crops.

Life is peaceful on a summer day in the countryside. However, traditional village life is under threat across Russia.

CHERNOZEM COUNTRY

Only about 13 percent of the Russian Federation is given over to agriculture because many regions are unsuitable due to climate or soil conditions. The most fertile areas stretch from southwestern Russia into Siberia. The rich, black soil, known as *chernozem*, is similar to that of the Canadian prairies and is ideal for growing wheat. Barley, oats, rye, and corn are also harvested. Root crops include sugar beets and potatoes. Pigs, cattle, and poultry are raised on large and small farms. While large amounts of meat are imported, grain exports make Russia the world's fifth largest shipper of wheat. The government is planning greater investment in agriculture in the future.

Ripe wheat stands are ready for the harvest in the Omsk region of southwestern Siberia.

CLIMATE FUTURE

The future for farming in Russia may depend on climate change. If the climate becomes warmer, as many scientists predict, new areas of the country could become suitable for farming. However, in other areas, drought may become more common and make farming very difficult or even turn land into desert.

At Ust-Barguzin, on the shores of Lake Baikal, anglers catch fish through holes in the ice.

ACROSS TWO CONTINENTS

The direct distance from Russia's westernmost territory, the Baltic enclave of Kaliningrad, to its easternmost Pacific coast is about 4,785 miles (7,700 km). The unity of the world's biggest country, the success of its governance, and its economy, all depend on how well the transport system can move people and goods across this vast section of the planet.

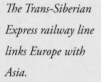

The Trans-Siberian Express railway line links Europe with Asia.

ROAD ROUTES

A network of highways links the cities of European Russia with each other and with Siberia. This comprises 482,000 miles (776,000 km) of paved roads in all. Although key routes have been upgraded in recent years, many country roads remain in poor condition and accidents are common.

BY TRAIN

Railways feature in many scenes from classical Russian literature and romantic films. The Trans-Siberian railway (see below) is famous worldwide. State-owned Russian Railways have the second largest rail network after the United States, with about 54,000 miles (87,000 km) of track. They carry 1.3 billion passengers a year and a vast amount of freight—from timber to coal. The railways constitute a major economy in themselves and employ about 950,000 people. Ten Russian cities now have rapid transit via metro or tram networks either already in service or under construction.

CROSSING RUSSIA

Moscow's Yaroslavsky station is the starting point for one of the world's most awe-inspiring journeys onboard the Trans-Siberian Express. Distant destinations include the port of Vladivostok on Russia's Pacific coast. Other Siberian networks link with Ulan Bator in Mongolia, Beijing in China, and Pyongyang in North Korea.

- How long is the railway? 5,770 miles (9,290 km) from Moscow to Vladivostok.

- What is the journey time? It takes 6 days and 4 hours from Moscow to Vladivostok—and trains generally arrive on time.

BY BOAT

Rivers and canals that can carry barges or shipping provide an even bigger transport network than the railways for both passengers and freight. They cross European Russia to link up with the Baltic, the White Sea, the Sea of Azov, and the Black Sea. Seaports are very important to a land giant such as Russia, but some Arctic harbors may be reached only with the help of icebreakers. In recent years, the decline in summer ice has allowed more ships to travel over the Arctic Ocean.

BY PLANE

Air travel has made the long and difficult journeys across Russia a thing of the past. Moscow is served by three large airports, Domodedovo International carries about 22.3 million passengers a year. Russia has 593 airports and a range of international and internal airlines. The largest and most profitable of these is Aeroflot, which was founded as the state airline in 1923.

The Russian ice-breaker 50 Let Pobedy *(50 Years of Victory).*

ENVIRONMENT AT RISK

Norilsk produces about 137,000 short tons (124,000 mt) of nickel and 335,000 short tons (304,000 mt) of copper a year.

The Arctic was once an unspoilt, icy wilderness. Norilsk in northern Siberia, population 175,000, is one of the coldest cities on the planet. And it is one of the most polluted. It is a center for mining nickel, and smelting fills the air with a toxic smog. Pollution has affected the health of the people. The ground is poisoned with heavy metals, and acid rain has destroyed large areas of forest. The mining company Norilsk Nickel states it will cut emissions at Norilsk by about two-thirds between 2015 and 2020, but lasting damage has already been done.

PROBLEMS PAST AND PRESENT

Russia's environmental problems have built up over many years. Leaking stocks of old pesticides have polluted land and water. Overgrazing and excessive logging have led to soil erosion. Mining and transport have damaged the tundra. The Barents Sea region of the Arctic has been irradiated by abandoned nuclear submarines and by years of weapons testing during the Cold War.

The Siberian crane is critically endangered.

ENERGY AND CLIMATE

Most scientists blame the release of carbon-based gases from power stations and factories for climate change. The Russian economy relies heavily on carbon-based fuels such as gas, oil, and coal. These are used to generate 68 percent of its electricity. Ten percent of Russia's energy comes from nuclear fuels—a resource that had a very poor safety record in the USSR. The 1986 explosion at the Chernobyl power plant (now in independent Ukraine) was probably the world's worst ever nuclear disaster. Scientists fear that global warming will eventually melt the Siberian permafrost. That could release large amounts of methane into the atmosphere and make the problem of global warming even worse.

A GREEN FUTURE?

Russia does have one renewable energy resource in abundance: water. Hydroelectric power generates 21 percent of the country's electricity. Other renewables, such as wind and solar power, are only now beginning to be developed. The Russian government plans to increase these to make up 4.5 percent of Russia's energy supply and to introduce other green policies such as energy efficiency and improved recycling, but it has a long way to go.

BEAR NECESSITIES

From tundra and forests to mountains and farmland, Russia is home to a rich variety of wildlife. More brown bears live in Russia than anywhere else on Earth and have long been seen as a symbol of the nation. Russia has its wildlife reserves, yet many species are still threatened by the spread of cities, the loss of habitat or prey animals, and widespread hunting.

- Species on the endangered list include the Siberian tiger, the Amur leopard, the snow leopard, the Russian lynx, and the Siberian crane.

- The loss of Arctic sea ice in summer months threatens the survival of walruses and polar bears.

Many of Moscow's commuters travel to work on an underground rail system. Metro is the third busiest rapid transit system in the word. It has 200 miles (325 km) of line and is growing. Some of its stations are very modern. Others date from the 1930s and are built in a lavish, ornate style with statues, fine tiles, and chandeliers.

MONEY MAGNET

In the 21st century, Moscow is dedicated to making money. An estimated 17 percent of all Russia's retail sales take place in the capital. About 20 percent of Russia's national GDP (gross domestic product—the value of all services and goods) comes from this one city. Moscow's factories produce chemicals, foodstuffs, textiles, cars, aerospace technology, vodka, and watches. The head offices of giant energy corporations, such as Gazprom, and new micro-electronic and software companies are also in Moscow. The city's new central business district is a center of finance, banking, and technology.

PAY

The average Moscow wage is $1,340 (46,000 rubles) per month, which is about twice as much as the figure for the rest of the country. The minimum legal wage in the city is $355 (12,200 rubles). At the other end of the scale, the city's many billionaires enjoy luxury lifestyles.

FINDING WORK

Moscow has the lowest unemployment rate in Russia, so it acts as a magnet for young migrant workers. Many are Tajiks, Uzbeks, and Kyrgyz from the Central Asian nations that broke away from the old Soviet Union in 1991. The migrants may work as cleaners, snow clearers, builders, or market traders. It is a hard life. For those who work illegally without the proper papers, arrest and deportation is a constant fear.

Built in the Soviet era, Moscow's classic Metro stations were designed to impress the world.

Migrant workers are ready for work at a Moscow construction site. Most migrant workers come from the former Soviet Asian republics, such as Turkmenistan.

The GUM building, by Red Square, is a symbol of Moscow's changing economy. It was a shopping arcade in the 1890s, a Soviet department store in the 1950s, and now is a classy shopping mall.

Farmers travel into Moscow to sell fruit and vegetables at the big open-air markets.

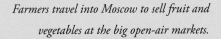

27

CHAPTER 3

RUSSIAN SOCIETY
JUSTICE AND THE LAW

Russian justice is often in the headlines. President Putin repeatedly makes stern calls for law and order. He rejects accusations made by his critics at home and by international organizations. The European Parliament places pressure on Russian courts and claims that human rights are being abused.

CRIME

Since the 1990s, Russia has seen an increase in homicide. Violent crimes often are related to the illegal trafficking of weapons and drugs, such as heroin, by criminal organizations and gangs. Behind the crime statistics are ongoing social problems such as poverty, alcoholism, and homelessness. Vulnerable social groups, such as abused women, homosexuals, and racial minorities, feel they are not properly protected by the law or by the justice system.

This is the Moscow headquarters of the Federal Security Service (FSB), which deals with surveillance, border controls, and organized crime.

PUNISHMENT

Most court cases go through the district-based People's Courts. Trials are based more upon direct questioning of the accused than on debate between prosecuting and defending lawyers. The use of juries is limited, and acquittals are very rare. The prison regime is very tough. Russia has a high number of prisoners in jail, third only after China and the United States. The law allows capital punishment, but no one has been executed since 1996.

POLICE AND STATE SECURITY

The Russian police used to be called the militia. In 2011, they were renamed, reorganized as a federal force, and given a pay raise to stamp out widespread corruption and improve their public image. State security is the responsibility of the Federal Security Service.

THE DEATH OF SERGEI MAGNITSKY

The strange case of Sergei Magnitsky has highlighted problems in the Russian system of justice.

- **2007** Police raided the Moscow offices of a finance company. They took away documents. Later these came into the hands of criminals who used them to transfer ownership of the company to themselves. They then claimed a tax refund of $230 million. Accountant Magnitsky was called in by the finance company to investigate.

- **2008** Magnitsky completed his investigation and filed an official complaint. But he was arrested instead of the criminals and accused of tax evasion.

- **2009** Magnitsky was held in prison for nearly a year. He died before going on trial.

- **2010–11** Outrage at Magnitsky's death spread around the world. It grew into a full-scale international dispute at the government level. After investigations, various officials were removed from their jobs.

- **2012–13** The trial against Magnitsky was reopened, and he was found guilty of fraud. Critics said this was an attempt to intimidate future whistleblowers.

Special police round up terrorism suspects during a 2013 raid on a market in St. Petersburg.

RIGHTS OR WRONGS?

The conflict between government authority and human rights has a long history in Russia as in many parts of the world. Both tsarist and Soviet rulers were authoritarian and operated with secret police forces. Concerns remain that political opponents of the government or whistleblowers who expose corruption or crime may be targeted or killed by criminals, security agents, or police.

KNOWLEDGE AND HEALTH

September 1 is Knowledge Day in Russia and the first day of the new school year. Children bring flowers for the teacher. The school year has four terms. School starts each day at 8:00 a.m. and ends about 2:00 p.m. Education has long been highly valued in Russia, and 99.6 percent of the adult population can read and write.

GOING TO SCHOOL

Russian schooling demands 11 years of compulsory education. Four years are spent in primary, five in secondary, and two in high school. All three levels often are housed in the same building. Some children go to preschool classes before the age of six. The state provides free education. However, since the 1990s, private schools have been introduced for those who can afford to pay the fees.

COLLEGE SHAKE-UP

Higher education includes vocational training colleges and universities. These institutions are both public and private. After the Soviet era, more teenagers wanted to go on to college. As the number of universities grew rapidly, the standards began to slide. In 2013, a new program was introduced to close failing colleges and channel funds to the top performers. Improving scientific research is a priority.

Another year means a fresh start at this Moscow school, and is marked by bouquets for the teachers.

Lomonosov Moscow State University is the oldest and largest college in Russia.

A Russian nurse holds a newborn baby. Today's Russia has a very low rate of population growth.

HEALTH ISSUES

In the 1950s, Russians could expect to live longer than Americans. In the 1990s, a Russian's life expectancy fell dramatically as the Soviet social welfare system was cut drastically. Today, life expectancy is creeping up again—76 for women and 64 for men. The sharp difference between the two sexes has been attributed to drinking habits. Life expectancy is still low when compared with 82 for women and 77 for men in the U.S. Major health risks include cancer and heart disease from smoking, and damage to the liver and heart caused by alcohol abuse.

MEDICINE IN RUSSIA

National health care is partly funded by compulsory insurance plans and partly by the taxpayer. Private treatment is now available. Russia has a very high ratio of doctors and hospital beds to the population. However, the organization of health care has been poor and government funding has lagged far behind the countries of the West. Putin's government is now putting serious investment into health care and modernizing the service, but it will take some years for things to improve.

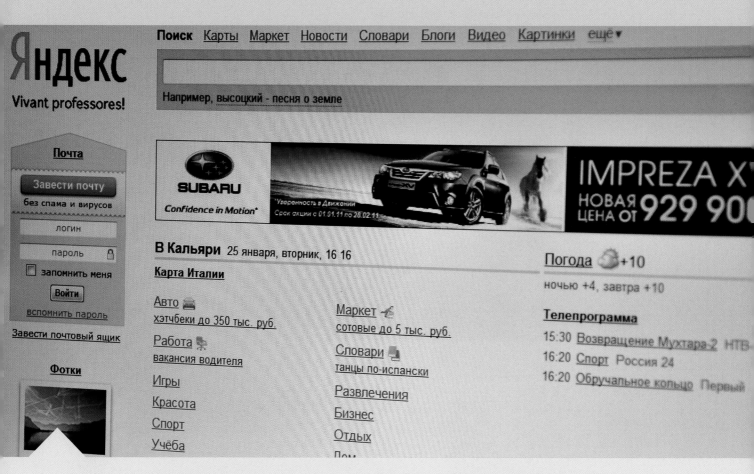

The Yandex search engine is the most popular in Russia and has a 64 percent share of the market.

Russia is part of the digital revolution that has swept the world. Telecommunications and information technology have had a great effect on the BRICS countries. It can bypass many of the problems associated with poor infrastructure and long-distance communication. Russia has 44 million landline phones and about 102 million cellphones, of which smartphones make up 37 percent.

ONLINE IN RUSSIA

Of the 70 million Internet users in Russia, eight in ten users log on to social-networking sites. Russian-based sites such as VK and Odnoklassiki are popular with Russian speakers in Russia and abroad. The top search engine is run by the Russian company Yandex.

CENSORSHIP

From 2011 to 2013 the Internet has been widely used to organize and coordinate protests about disputed election results and against government policies said to be authoritarian. However, Russia, unlike China, has not attempted to seal off international political influence with a firewall. New laws passed in 2012 do blacklist certain sites. These include sites that may promote social problems such as drug abuse. These laws were used to shut down, briefly, a satirical Russian website called Lurkmore.

A FREE PRESS?

While the traditional press is in decline in many Western countries, Russian newspapers still boast a yearly circulation of about 8.2 billion copies. Russia has more journalists than any other country in the world. With little formal censorship, the government will brief, bribe, and intimidate the press to get a story across. Journalists who investigate criminal activity or corruption risk being attacked or murdered. The writer Anna Politovskaya was shot dead outside her flat by unknown persons in 2006. She had uncovered breaches of human rights during the conflict in Chechnya and was a fearless critic of Vladimir Putin.

A newspaper and magazine kiosk shows the variety of publications for sale in Russia.

The recording studio of a popular Russian TV talent show called KVN.

TV REALITY

Russia is a nation of avid television viewers. Comedies, crime thrillers, and game and reality shows win big audiences. Russia has six federal television channels, many more regional and local broadcasters, and hundreds of radio stations. The state-funded multi-language international television network, Russia Today (RT), has been very successful, attracting a worldwide audience of 550 million people. About two-thirds of all media are owned or part-owned by the state. Most political programs play it safe. Many younger people have deserted the mainstream media for Internet viewing.

ARTS, MUSIC, AND SPORTS

Russian people have a long tradition of costume and embroidery, decoration and woodcarving, playing musical instruments such as the three-stringed balalaika, and energetic folk dances. When it comes to fine painting, music, dance, literature, and movies, Russia has an extraordinary record.

RUSSIAN GENIUS

Russia's artistic tradition dates back to the richly ornamented religious icons of the Middle Ages. The 18th century saw the founding of classical ballet companies such as the Mariinsky and the Bolshoi. It was also the start of the world's great art collections at the Hermitage museum in St. Petersburg. The 19th century was a golden era with stirring symphonies and concertos of composer Pyotr Ilyich Tchaikovsky. Writers such as Fyodor Dostoyevsky and Leo Tolstoy introduced Russia to the world. The turbulent 20th century yielded yet more artistic creativity from the films of Sergei Eisenstein to the music of Sergei Prokofiev and Dmitri Shostakovich.

PRANKS AND PUNKS

Since the fall of the Soviet Union, Russian artists and musicians have found new directions, testing out the new nature of political power and wealth, and using video and other new media to get their message across. Satire, shock, and rebellion have been common themes. Crazed perfomance art from Oleg Kulik and a feminist punk band called Pussy Riot caught international attention. In 2012 the band outraged Russian authorities by performing "Punk Prayer: Mother of God Chase Putin Away" in Moscow's Cathedral of Christ the Savior. Accused of religious hatred, the band was sentenced to two years in a prison camp. In May 2013, one member, Maria Alyokhina, went on hunger strike when she was refused parole.

Out to shock, the feminist punk band Pussy Riot perform in Moscow.

TIME OUT

To many Russians, performance does not mean theater or ballet, but it's how well their favorite team is doing. Soccer is the most popular spectator sport. With huge interest in the national team, the 2018 FIFA World Cup will be hosted by Russia. In recent years, the game's fortunes have depended on backing from billionaires. The money can propel minor clubs, such as FC Anzhi Makhachkala, to fame with international signings. Other top sports in Russia are ice hockey and basketball.

Russia's national ice hockey team takes on Canada at a world championship contest.

RELIGION AND CUSTOMS

Christianity came to the Slavs from Constantinople (modern Istanbul) over 1,100 years ago. It was a cornerstone of the Russian state under the tsars. However, Soviet communism was officially atheist. It was hostile to all religions and dismissed them as superstitions used by the powerful to hold back social progress. Many churches were destroyed or taken over. Although religions were not banned, believers were often persecuted or sent to labor camps.

OLD WAYS

Many Russians remain atheists today, but the Russian Orthodox Church is thriving again. It is supported by 40 percent of the population. While major churches in the big cities have been rebuilt or restored, many rural churches remain in a dilapidated state. Controversially, the leaders of the Russian Orthodox Church are as close to Putin as the leaders were to the tsars in the old days. The church tends toward pro-government, nationalist, and conservative. Religious education has been made a compulsory part of the school curriculum. Some Russians are members of other Christian churches and sects.

In a Russian Orthodox wedding ceremony, the candles represent the light of Christ. The crowns mark the union of man and woman.

One of the largest mosques in Russia is at the heart of Grozny, Chechnya.

MULTI-FAITH

Nearly 7 percent of all Russians are Muslims. Most live in the Caucasus Mountains and in the Central Asian regions of the federation. Jews once played a major role in Russian society. But over the centuries, many fled persecution in Russia and settled elsewhere in Europe or in the United States. Beginning in the 1970s, many Jews emigrated to Israel. Many remaining Jews are secular rather than religious. Buddhism has followers in some southern regions. In recent years, there has been a revival of interest in pagan beliefs held by the Slavs and people of Siberia in ancient times.

FESTIVALS AND FEASTS

- Christmas Day is celebrated on January 7.

- Malenitsa is celebrated in the seventh week before Easter. Pancakes are made and there are sleigh rides, snowball fights, and the burning of a straw effigy.

- Real eggs, hand-painted in beautiful patterns and colors, are exchanged at Easter. Food treats include a round cheesecake with fruits and almonds. It is known as pashka (the same as the word for Easter).

- St. Petersburg is so far north that it barely gets dark at night around midsummer. These "White Nights" are celebrated with music, dancing, and boat rides.

ENJOYING THE CITY

How do Muscovites relax? On a hot summer's day, they may take a boat ride on the Moscow River. Many go swimming in the water, despite the pollution. Some even swim in the river on freezing days in the winter. More sensible people fish—through holes bored in the ice.

MEETING PLACES

In 2011, Moscow's Gorky Park, a former fair site, was redeveloped as a fashionable meeting place. It offers ice skating, salsa dancing classes, and an open-air theater. Other city parks and green spaces are also being refurbished. Moscow's *banyas* (bathhouses) are traditional saunas for luxuriating in steam before being beaten with a branch of oak leaves! Men and women have separate areas where they can meet up to socialize and have a drink.

ENTERTAINMENT

The Old Moscow Circus opened on Tsvetnoy Boulevard in 1880. Its clowns have continued to entertain the public ever since. Moscow's theaters offer opera, classic drama, and the world-famous Bolshoi ballet. Sports fans are fortunate in Moscow. It has five of Russia's top soccer teams: Spartak, Lokomotiv, CSKA, FC Moscow, and Dynamo. The city is also home to the nation's Luzhniki Stadium.

FOOD AND CELEBRATION

The growing wealth in the city has changed Muscovites' attitude to eating. Many now attend food festivals or dine out at fancy restaurants run by celebrity chefs. Every type of international cuisine is available in the city. Traditional Russian cooking includes dishes such as *borscht* (beet soup), *shchi* (cabbage soup), beef Stroganoff (sautéed strips of meat served with sour cream), Moscow chicken (creamy, served with onions and mushrooms), *blinis* (thin pancakes), and *pirozhki* (glazed buns with fillings such as mushroom, egg, beef, salmon, or fruit). Family gatherings, weddings, and anniversaries bring out the Muscovites' love of celebration. These include hours of feasting, drinking, dancing, intense conversation, and discussion around the dining tables.

Moscow's classiest banya, the Sanduny, dates back to 1808. It has been restored to its original splendor. It includes a magnificent swimming pool.

The grand Pushkin Museum of Fine Arts shows European masterpieces. The State Tretyakov Gallery houses the nation's most important collection of Russian paintings.

Hunting for a bargain? The bustling Izmailovo market offers cheap clothing, handicrafts, antiques, souvenirs such as Russian dolls, samovars (traditional urns for making tea), and street snacks such as kebabs and samosas.

Skaters take to the ice in Moscow's Gorky Park, which was recently restyled as a fashionable recreation center.

Black caviar is made from the eggs of a fish called the sturgeon. Caviar can be served with a blini and a glass of champagne—a very expensive delicacy!

RUSSIA INTERNATIONAL

Today's generation of politicians grew up during the Cold War. In those days, people in the West used to say that Russia was "behind the Iron Curtain" meaning it was cut off from the rest of the world.

Tourists flock to see Russia's historic buildings, including the Hermitage in St. Petersburg.

BRAVE NEW WORLD

Today, all that has changed. Western tourists and businesspeople enjoy moving freely about the streets of Moscow and St. Petersburg. Ordinary Russians now travel abroad as tourists. Moscow's rich invest overseas in property, soccer clubs, and media. Russia's oil wealth, rather than its military power, has made it a big player in international politics.

A GAME OF CHESS

Cold War attitudes still linger on both sides. Putin and his prime minister, Medvedev, are quick to defend what they see as Russia's national interests. In 2012, Russia spoke out against U.S. plans to install a missile defense system in Poland, which Russia regarded as a threat to its security. In recent years, Russia's relations with Iran and Syria, a former ally, have worried Western governments.

Russia's record on human rights is another recurring issue in international politics. The death of whistleblower Sergei Magnitsky in 2009 while he was in a Russian prison (see page 29) has triggered an ongoing dispute between Russia and the United States.

THE FUTURE

Closer contact and a great deal of genuine cooperation among the United States, the European Union, and Russia have made the world a safer place. As part of BRICS, Russia has been building bridges in Asia, Africa, and South America.

Is Russia misrepresented in the Western media and unfairly criticized? Many Russians believe so. It is true that human rights abuses, severe environmental problems, corruption, and the gap between the richest and poorest in society are not unique to Russia. These issues are in the news all over the world and may be applied to some of Russia's critics. In whichever country these problems arise, they have to be dealt with for the sake of a future that actually works. The country has no shortage of young Russians who are ready to take up that challenge.

U.S. President Barack Obama and Russian Prime Minister Dimitry Medvedev. Relations between the two world powers have improved since the Cold War, but tensions remain.

WHICH WAY FORWARD?

In 1939, Winston Churchill, an English statesman, said that Russia was "a riddle, wrapped in a mystery, wrapped in an enigma." His phrase is similar to the Russian matryoshka dolls. Each doll contains smaller models of itself. They are often painted in the likeness of Russia's leaders, present to past, one inside the other.

RUSSIA'S MANY COLORS

The multilayered nature of the new Russia can be seen at parades and demonstrations. The national flag is red, white, and blue. Red is for revolution with a hammer-and-sickle emblem representing the workers. The black, gold, and white flags of the 19th century empire were flown by royalists and ultra-nationalists. White ribbons are widely worn by opponents of Vladimir Putin.

PAST LESSONS?

Putin urges his followers to be inspired by Russian history, but that raises many conflicting ideas. The motto of Tsar Nicholas II was "Orthodoxy, autocracy, and nationality." The Communist leader Lenin said, "Freedom in capitalist society always remains . . . Freedom for slave owners." Reformer Gorbachev called for "Restructuring and Openness." Those voting for the first time face many decisions if they are to decide the best way forward.

A nest of matryoshka dolls represents Russian leaders (left to right): Nikita Khrushchev, Leonid Brezhnev, Mikhail Gorbachev, Boris Yelstsin, Dimitry Medvedev, and Vladimir Putin.

After the "Last Bell" ceremony, high school graduates head out to have some fun. What will the future hold for them?

VOTING FOR HOPE

Russia has great economic potential if it is managed wisely. Having learned how to endure a harsh climate and adapt to a challenging landscape, its people are tough. They have survived authoritarian rule and fought off invasions. Their writers and musicians have inspired the world. They live in the largest country on the planet and, if its landscape can be preserved, one of awe-inspiring beauty.

A symbol of old Russia, the 12th century Church of the Intercession rises from the banks of the River Neri.

GLOSSARY

acid rain acidic rainfall, polluted by sulfur dioxide or nitrogen oxides

acquittal being found not guilty of a crime

ally a country that supports another

armaments weapons of war

atheist not believing in a god or gods

authoritarian demanding loyalty to the government above individual freedom

autocracy rule by a monarch or leader with absolute power

balalaika three-stringed musical instrument with a triangular body

Bolsheviks members of a faction in the Russian Social Democratic Labor Party, which seized power in the October Revolution of 1917 and later became the Communist Party of the Soviet Union

BRICS a grouping of nations with rapidly developing economies—Brazil, Russia, India, China, and South Africa

capital punishment the death penalty

capitalism an economic system based on private ownership and the accumulation of wealth

circulation the number of published newspapers or magazines copies distributed

civil war a war fought between people from the same country

climate change a major change in weather patterns and conditions measured over a long period

Cold War a period of great international tension between the United States and its allies on one side, and communist countries such as the Soviet Union and China on the other

collective a working enterprise shared by a number of people or groups

communism a political system based upon rule by a political party representing the working class

conservative supporting tradition, opposing change

corruption dishonest practice, such as bribery of officials

Cyrillic a system of writing based on Greek letters, which evolved into the Russian alphabet

elite a small group of powerful, wealthy, or talented people

emissions gases or other substances given out by a process, such as pollution from a power station

enclave a territory of one country that is surrounded by the lands of another

erosion the wearing down of soil or rock by wind, water, ice, or heat

ethnic group a group of people sharing ancestry, customs, and culture

faction a group of people with shared political aims, often within a larger political grouping

federal representing the Russian Federation as a whole, rather than individual regions or cities.

GDP gross domestic product, the value of goods and services produced within a country over a given period of time

global warming a long-term increase in Earth's temperature

head of state the senior person representing a nation, such as a president or a monarch

heavy metals a term often used to describe toxic metals that cause pollution

homicide the killing of another human being.

human rights the basic conditions required to ensure life, liberty, and justice.

hydroelectric power derived from turbines driven by water

icebreaker a ship designed to force its way through frozen sea

icon a religious painting produced as an act of devotion

infrastructure basic systems such as roads, drainage, water and electricity mains, transportation, and communications

irradiate to contaminate with radioactive material

life expectancy the average period one can expect to live

methane a chemical compound found in natural gas

militia a citizen fighting force, formerly the name of the police in Russia

minimum wage the lowest wage that can be legally paid in a country or region

minority an ethnic group or class

of people who make up less than half the total population

missile defense a system designed to attack or prevent incoming enemy missiles

oligarch a member of a ruling elite or, in modern Russia, any individual with great power and wealth

pagan pre-Christian religions related to nature and the countryside

peasant a poor rural worker

permafrost in Arctic lands, a layer of soil that remains frozen all year

population density the number of people living within a given unit of area

renewable any form of energy that comes from a source that is continually replenished, such as wind or the Sun, and not from finite resources, such as coal, oil, or uranium

republic in Russia, an administrative division with a high proportion of non-ethnic Russians

sect a religious grouping or faction

secular non-religious

serf a laborer who has to work the land for his master and has no right to move away or seek other employment

smelt to obtain metal by heating ore in a furnace

steppe grassland or prairie

taiga a northern forest environment dominated by pines, spruces, and larches

tsar a Russian emperor

tundra treeless plains and mountains bordering the polar regions

Turkic an ethnic group or language originating in Central Asia

ultra-nationalist someone who believes in the superiority of their nation

FURTHER INFORMATION

BOOKS

Countries Around the World: Russia, Jilly Hunt (Raintree, 2012)

Countries in Our World: Russia, Galya Ransome (Smart Apple Media, 2010)

WEBSITES

www.bbc.com/news/world-europe-17839881
A profile of Russia, including facts and timeline.

www.russiapedia.rt.com/basic-facts-about-russia/
A useful summary of Russia today.

www.spartacus-educational.com/Russia.htm
Access to a wide-ranging series of articles and profiles from Russian history.

www.travel.nationalgeographic.com/travel/countries/russia-guide/
National Geographic's views of travel through Russia.

INDEX